YOU ARE SOMETHING NEW

life lessons to radically change

how you show up in business

Meg Seitz

Aurora Corialis Publishing

Pittsburgh, PA

YOU ARE SOMETHING NEW: LIFE LESSONS TO RADICALLY
CHANGE HOW YOU SHOW UP IN BUSINESS

Printed in the United States of America

Edited by: Greg Leatherman, Aurora Corialis Publishing

Cover Design: Karen Captline, BetterBe Creative

Paperback ISBN: 978-1-958481-19-6

Ebook ISBN: 978-1-958481-20-2

ABOUT THE COVER

The cover of this book features the Upper Antelope Canyon, which is a slot canyon east of LeChee, Ariz., on Navajo land. Navajo presence in the American Southwest dates to AD 1400.

In the Navajo language, this canyon is called *Tsé bighánílíní* which means "the place where water runs through rocks," as it was formed by generations of flash flooding.

It is well-known for the beams of sunlight that seep in from openings at the top of the canyon. Light beams in this canyon occur most often in summer; they start to peek into the canyon around the spring equinox each year (March 19–20) and disappear by October 20.

Praise for *You Are Something New*

"*You Are Something New* is an enthralling book that delivers on its promise to get you to pay more attention and learn from the world around you. Meg's generous heart and relentless desire to keep making a difference are perfectly expressed in this book. Here's what to expect: you'll occasionally chuckle, be stirred up, and definitely be left with lots of food for thought."

Daniel Adeyemi, Award-Winning Journalist & Two-Time Winner of the Peter Drucker Challenge

———

"Meg Seitz draws upon her life experiences to inspire people not only to be better business leaders, but also to be better people. She challenges the reader to examine their lives through a new worldview: do you know your "granite" foundational values, do you have the ability to be agile enough to change in the face of challenges, and are you brave enough to push yourself into overdrive when you need to. I have been inspired by working side-by-side with Meg and seeing how she embodies these traits, beliefs, and values. She does not just talk about them, she lives them. This book is for all readers from new leaders to the board room."

Marty Stowe, CEO, Spartan Leadership Consulting

———

"This is a must-read book for anyone seeking meaningful growth in business and life. While most business books offer generic advice, Meg digs deep into the genuine human side of leadership, blending artistry with real-life experiences to spark genuine transformation. The 'Prompts for Radical Change' at the end of each chapter will challenge you to think critically, see the world differently, and evolve into who you truly aspire to be."

Jennifer Blake Gluckow, Bestselling Author

for my family

FOREWORD

I met Meg Seitz in a world far from business—an independent school. We first spoke at a coffee shop one July afternoon because she had been hired to teach English, and I was fortunate to be her mentor. Not too far removed from completing her English degree at Kenyon College, she came south to Charlotte, NC, from Pittsburgh, Pa., excited to explore the world of teaching. I was prepared to guide her step by step in learning the complex and intricate art of teaching.

On the first day, I showed her how to use the copier and gave her a textbook. That was the extent of my mentoring duties. She needed no guidance. In her first month, Meg proved she was an excellent teacher; her brand of teaching was a refreshing change from others just entering the profession. She transcended the typical system-bound ideologies ingrained in teachers entering education through the typical channels. Through every lesson, every novel, and every assignment, she helped students understand that storytelling is foundational to learning what it means to be human. She understood that in business, in medicine, in art, in technology, and in law, stories connect us to people and ideas.

Eventually, Meg left to pursue other career goals and to earn her MBA from Wake Forest University, and just as she did not confine herself within the typical norms and behaviors of academia, she also abandoned the system-bound thinking of business. Instead, she focused on being a creative thought leader.

One of Meg's superpowers is embracing the harmony of "and" instead of accepting the dichotomy of "or." Other people either know or have questions. Meg knows and questions. Other people either take action or deliberate carefully. Meg takes action *and* deliberates carefully. Other people consider tradition or challenge norms, but Meg is both an upholder and an innovator. She personifies her values through **toth shop,** which is a highly successful company that "brings artistry to business." Meg named her business after one of her great-grandmothers, Elizabeth Toth Doczy, a fearless risk-taker who came to America in 1912 at the age of 19, despite knowing no one and not speaking English. That same moxie and daring runs through Meg's veins (think Virginia Woolf meets Lady Gaga, with a healthy dose of style).

Meg may have left a high school classroom, but she continues to teach. She has taught graduate classes as an adjunct faculty member at Queens University of Charlotte and an instructor for Davidson College's Hurt Hub for Innovation and Entrepreneurship. She has written successful children's books about business and entrepreneurship.

This book is an extension of Meg's passion for teaching. It will not provide blueprints, checklists, forecasts, or data. In fact, you will not even find those words on these pages. While Meg acknowledges their importance, she resists speaking in absolutes, which can often frustrate people when they try a "one size fits all" formula that doesn't work for their business. Meg's vignettes invite us to view our business from a different seat in the room. Her stories don't provide generic answers; they lead us to ask informed questions, so we can consider our own "what ifs" and "what nows."

Meg Seitz wants to help those of us who wish to bring artistry to our personal and professional lives. For example, she teaches us how to pay attention to negative space, a technique where artists focus on the space between and around an object (the object being the positive space). This technique requires the artist to observe an object through the shape found in the negative space, and not just by observing the object itself. It seems paradoxical, doesn't it? To see what is there, artists consider what is *not* there. Paying attention to how positive and negative spaces interact helps an artist create balance. This book challenges readers to look for the negative space in our personal and professional lives. How does that negative space emphasize what is already there? How can we use the positive and negative to achieve a balance? Observing and asking questions allows us to examine our potential or discover new opportunities.

Meg wants us to see that we have the power to write – and rewrite – our story as many times as needed. This book is like our own pair of ruby slippers, reminding us we have had the power all along.

Ginger Holloway

Teacher-Leader

October 2023

TABLE OF CONTENTS

'Forget the former things;

do not dwell on the past.

See I am doing a new thing!

Now it springs up;

do you not perceive it?

I am making a way in the wilderness

and streams in the wasteland.'

Isaiah 43:18-19

INTRODUCTION

Does anyone, anywhere ever really excel at the good ol' "give-us-a-fun-fact-about-yourself" ice breaker question? I mean, seriously, is there a *worse* question?

If you're human, you've answered that question at some point. Chances are, you rolled your eyes internally the second someone shared the prompt. We all do. And, as much as we try, no one really has a memorable answer.

When I attended business school orientation, they threw that question at us on the first day. It was naturally tied to giving our names and what we did professionally. Then came the lay-up: We each had to share the dreaded fun fact about ourselves. As you might expect, answers were typically a ten-second spiel about having run a marathon or just gotten married.

One of our classmates gave his name and job title, and then his fun fact: "I'm consistently inconsistent." Everyone kind of chuckled to themselves.

Over two years, however, we found that Paul was right. The guy was a smart, high-performer — a stock trader by day, an MBA student with all of us by night — but he was consistently inconsistent. He was sometimes in class; sometimes not; he'd sometimes show up to drinks and dinner after class; oftentimes not. You just never really knew what Paul was up to. He didn't really care either. Yet, he knew exactly who he was; he told us that the first day. What was initially a laugh was probably the truest, least-bullshit answer to the fun fact ask.

As I've grown older, I've come to realize something about his answer. We all are. Every person on Earth is consistently inconsistent, in one way or another.

At first glance, it's a negative thing. I mean, who wants to be consistently inconsistent? Am I proud of the fact I ran on the treadmill three days in a row, then pulled a muscle, and skipped five days? Or that I said I'd post on LinkedIn every day for a month, and then got distracted one morning, and forgot for two days, and then two days again? It's no one's goal to be consistently inconsistent.

But it does make you human. *One hundred percent human.*

If you look up the definition of "consistency," you'll find definitions having to do with agreement or harmony; or firmness and density. If you look up the word "consistent," you'll get definitions like "unchanging" or "steady"; and "doing something in the same way over time," "to be fair or accurate."

At the end of the day, do we want to be that level of consistent or unchanged? Probably not.

From the get-go, my career has been a scrappy collection of experiences or jobs; classes, courses, or certifications; people and teams; opportunities and risks.

The throughline has been me; it's been a very human journey.

Because I change constantly; I am something new all the time.

That's true for all of us. Because life happens. We graduate, we move, we start relationships, we end relationships, we travel and see the world, we come home and feel different, people are born into this world; others leave it.

Things and people and experiences change us all the time. If we let them.

Back in college, I had a theater professor who, after every scene, followed our class applause with two questions: "What'd ya see? What'd ya think?"

I don't think we ask ourselves or each other those questions enough. For example, a couple of months ago, I was talking to a friend who just ran her first marathon. Forever curious and trying to connect dots, I asked how her training and running experience changed how she thinks about work.

"I hadn't really thought about that," she answered.

When we allow ourselves to see the cross pollination of experiences, everything becomes something new to use in and for our lives.

I wrote this book for a couple of reasons.

First, after reading almost every business book on the market for more than a decade, I decided I wanted to provide the next generation of leaders, as well as stalled leaders, with an alternative to the traditional business book. Something that felt like both artistry and business. Something that delivered two values that the world and its people are most void of right now: Paying attention and thinking critically.

I find that paying attention and thinking critically impacts how I show up in the world as me, but also how I show up in the world as a business owner, which is really, truly the next frontier of this kind of thinking. I'd like to see more humanity in how we partner with people, how we do business, how we create an impact and legacy.

Forever a teacher, I realized that to do that, I need to show some examples of what paying attention and thinking critically looks like. And that it's oftentimes not only found in the beautiful, successful, positive moments. Sometimes, it's found in the frustrations, the forehead slap moments, the hard stuff... Also, though some of these stories involve travel and seeing the world, a lot happens in the average, everyday moments.

The overarching call to action is this: Pay attention.

Paying attention is hard, especially if you have a cell phone, which at this point, is almost everyone on planet Earth. To help with that, I end each chapter with 'prompts for radical change,' which are questions to get you thinking, writing, talking — perhaps with others, but, most importantly, with yourself.

My micro wish for you is that you read this and start to see your world differently.

My big wish is that you realize you are consistently inconsistent, and that's a good thing. Because when you're constantly evolving, so is everything about your world—your work, your relationships, and your impact. It changes how you show up, not only for the world, but even more so for yourself.

Whether you're a business leader, a school leader, or the bold and brave leader of your own life, I hope this different perspective will bring more humanity, grace, and artistry to your leadership.

Artistry and business are everywhere; go find it, connect the dots, see what happens.

And remember: You really, truly are something new every single day. Live, work, and play like that.

Lastly, I have a personal request. Those of you whom I know and who have read my work over the last 15 years across the *Huffington Post* or LinkedIn or the **toth shop** newsletter, will recognize some stories. Whether they're completely new to you or you're hearing it again with "new" ears and eyes, I hope you have an aha moment. And, if you do have an aha moment while reading this book, I hope you'll reach out and share that insight with me. We get smarter and sharper when we share with each other. You can email me at meg@tothshop.com.

Can't wait to hear from you.

Love,

Meg

CHAPTER ONE:
find your solid foundation

My sister, Maret, and I spent a lot of the summer of 1994 with our next-door neighbor, Marsha. Our grandmother was sick, and our mom—Gram and Poppy's only child and caregiver—lived a nonstop, grueling cycle of driving our red Volvo 240 for 45 minutes between home and the hospital. Marsha and her husband, Rod, were a blessing to our family. We'd carry a stack of VHS tapes to their house, talk, laugh, make popcorn, drink Dr. Pepper out of glass bottles, and watch movies together. Sometimes we'd watch *The Andy Griffith Show.*

Marsha loved that show, but at our ages—me, eleven; Maret, six—we didn't get it. We'd hear that opening whistle and almost roll our eyes. We'd watch it, though, and she'd watch *Free Willy* with us later.

When you're eleven and six, and it's the early '90s, that's an even exchange.

Years later, when I heard Andy Griffith died, I stood there for a minute and remembered Marsha's love for that show, and how much their family meant to our family.

I absorbed a lot as to how to be a good neighbor, a good friend, a good person. Almost 20 years later, and after at least seven moves between both families, we remain dear friends.

One year, for one of Maret's twentysomething birthdays, she wanted the two of us to drive from Charlotte to Mount Airy, NC, to explore. Andy Griffith grew up in Mount Airy, and he chose to loosely base the show's fictional town, Mayberry, on it.

It all started at "Wally's Service Station." We scheduled a tour in "Andy's squad car," which was a 1960 Ford Galaxie 500, naturally. A bell jingled when we opened the "service station's" front door, and our tour guide, who was approximately 75 years old, dropped whatever he was doing, hustled over to grab the car's keys, led us to the car, and opened the car doors for us. We yanked the doors shut using a wee bit more muscle than we did for my 2012 Jetta.

"Does he need us to verify we signed up for this? I'm assuming we pay for this later?" Maret and I mouthed to each other.

I love stuff like this. I was thinking about who I couldn't wait to talk to about this whole experience as I Instagrammed pictures of my sister sitting in the front seat. Our tour guide flipped on the siren. We giggled like kids. He told classic, clean, old-man jokes. He shared anecdotes about the show and "Andy." He drove us to a granite rock quarry. We learned that Mount Airy's North Carolina Granite Corporation supplies more granite worldwide than any other quarry.

I slouched in the backseat of a 1960s squad car Googling "granite." Facts about this hard, tough, durable, quality rock appeared. *Yosemite National Park's Half Dome is a granite dome. Mount Airy. North Carolina Granite Corporation. Full in operation since 1889. World's largest open-face granite quarry.*

Open face means ground level. Granite currently left in the Mount Airy quarry will last another 500 years. 500 years. That's just cool.

The squad car pulled down the hill from the quarry and chugged back through downtown Mount Airy. He parked alongside a suburban street curb and stick-shift-jerked the car into park. He pointed across the street to a house. Like a lot of local architecture constructed during the same era, this particular house was built with slabs of granite. It's mid-size and regal, practical, and luxurious. He said they stopped building like "this"—with granite—when materials got too expensive during the Great Depression.

"They don't make them like this anymore," he said.

We all just kind of sat there staring at this house. *They don't make them like this anymore.*

"Them" like houses, public buildings, churches, small towns, cities, but also homes, communities, foundations, values.

I needed to stop being a 21st century jerk. I needed to get off the phone. I needed to bring to a screeching halt my obnoxious use of quotation marks to describe this place as if it's not real. It's real. This place is just about as real as it gets.

In that moment, I thought: "I want a granite house." Or maybe, I want what a granite house signifies. What this town inspires. What that television show instills. I want that good, old-fashioned, classic, American experience way of doing things. It's no coincidence that this town, built beside a rock-solid, high-quality, long-enduring, almost ageless quarry inspired a television show and a way of doing things that is, in fact, just that: high-quality, long-enduring, almost ageless.

Where did the granite houses go?

I get the idea of change or technological innovation or essential cost-cutting for production or labor. I was sitting in the back of a 1960 Ford Galaxie 500 wearing stretchy, skinny denim and imitation-Wayfarer-sunglasses-probably-made-in-China pattering on my iPhone, for crying out loud.

But where did the granite houses, the solid foundations, the non-negotiable values, the people, places, and businesses who know who they are and stick to that go? Where do you shape a house or building with a quality product that lasts? Where do you drop what you're doing when someone walks in the door because they're a real, live person? Where do you trust people to pay after the tour?

We stayed in Mount Airy for the rest of the day. We ate pork rib sandwiches off paper plates and drank coffee out of Styrofoam cups. We split a chocolate milkshake while sitting on red, pleather swivel chairs at a diner counter. We picked up a newsletter from The Andy Griffith Rerun Fan Club.

We met a barber who's been in business since the late 1940s. His entourage of older gentlemen with thick, charming, southern drawls hung out in chairs along his shop's wall. They asked where we drove in from and if either of us were married, and when we each said, "Charlotte" and "no," they said there are plenty of men in Charlotte.

"It could happen tomorrow," one said.

There's no question that this town loves Andy Griffith. It's familial pride. But I think, more importantly, this town and other towns like it embody everything that's good, solid, and unassuming about American culture—and how we choose to treat each other.

Yes, the world is changing quickly. But when you're rooted in the solid foundation that built this country—people and places — you've got growth potential. Because it lasts... this granite, this community, this television show, this way of life. There are always enough of the right people around who care to preserve that which is good. You just have to find those people. Their legacy outlives everything else, even the granite.

Several years ago, I pitched a foundational messaging package to a client. In that package, our team works with their team to think through, write, and refine the storytelling pieces that we think are essential to how people do business. I'm talking about elements like: mission, vision, and core values. Let's call it the granite of the business, i.e., the content elements that serve as the foundation for decision making across sales and marketing; concept, design, and launch; communication and operations; and, well, *everything*. In theory, those pieces serve as the purpose, the big why—why we're doing this work, why we care, and why we keep pushing forward.

As I explained the package and the work we'd do with him and his team on mission, vision, and values, the client cut me off mid-sentence.

"We don't need the fluff," he snapped flippantly.

Ask yourself. Are the mission, vision, and core values of an organization just fluff, or are they foundational?

Some might say, "Well, it's a matter of opinion as to the importance of those elements," and I would agree. It is an opinion. Some businesses get it; some businesses don't. We have plenty of clients who pause processes because they need to get clear on who they are and what they do. We also work with founders who are fanatical about getting the wording just right in their mission statement or their vision; teams who keep pushing almost as though it was a workout to narrow their ten core values down to five, or even three. These are people, teams, and businesses craving that connection to a solid foundation. It sometimes reminds me of the scene in the movie *Annie Hall* when Jeff Goldblum's character leaves a sunny Los Angeles pool party to make a phone call and says to whomever is on the other end of the telephone line, "I forgot my mantra."

What I've found is when the people behind businesses and brands are unclear on the foundational elements, they're unclear on everything to come. When there's no granite, there's no place to build a future.

Granted, it's hard to lay a foundation with granite. It's big; it's heavy; it's expensive. When you're just starting your career or your business, it's hard to commit to granite.

On the flip side, in the absence of granite, comes grit and scrappiness and stick–to–itiveness. When a team is trying to cobble together the foundation, but they persevere in the process, that stands for a lot.

A solid foundation doesn't always have to be something physical; it can be an experience. *Phantom of the Opera* didn't run on Broadway for more than 30 years because it lacked a solid foundation. There was "granite" in its music and lyrics, its casting, and its message. When the chandelier dropped and that opening music came on, it was granite of an entirely different sort. In that sense, a foundation can be seen and felt, even when it's not entirely visible.

See, the choice to build a foundation of granite, whether for a house or a team, is really about confidence. It's a commitment to quality. You don't move forward with granite because you want to cut corners. You're confident enough to go for it.

In that case, granite is a mindset. Are you interested in building from a solid foundation—whether investing in materials or talent—or are you building with an attitude that your foundation is just fluff standing in the way of money or power or looking like a bigger deal than you are?

Building a foundation doesn't happen overnight. It takes time. It also evolves and changes; transforms and morphs. What does stay the same is a deep need to keep coming back to a center that is a constant. But center and constant are two different things. One is the place from which you operate, the other the rhythm. From kindergarten through twelfth grade, was my mom there at the house for us every day after school? Yes. She was both the center and the constant; the place and the rhythm. (And, yes, it was both a privilege and a gift for us.)

The big question is this: Which approach lasts longer? Which approach makes the builder feel prouder and more fulfilled?

prompts for radical change

In case you missed it, this is a conversation about operating from a solid foundation. That foundation can be how you operate personally, from which you build your business and impact, as well as for yourself and how you show up as a leader.

- What does "foundation" mean to you? What's your relationship with the concept?
- What's the granite, i.e., *the solid foundation,* in your life?
- When was the last time you called something fluff—and missed the boat completely?

- When was the last time you explored, and stumbled on something—maybe art, a building, a performance—that felt like it was built from a solid foundation, literally or figuratively?
- Where did the granite houses go?

CHAPTER TWO:
know your curiosity
overdrive mode

At 22 years old, I was fresh off an English degree from Kenyon College in Gambier, Ohio, and I was living at home trying to figure out my next move or, better said, my first move.

Just months before, on a hot Saturday morning in May, I was fortunate to be heralded into the real world with a now famous commencement address—"This is Water" by David Foster Wallace. If you haven't read it or heard it, I ask you to stop whatever you're doing right now, and go find it.

Though I could never do Foster Wallace's address justice, the one big thought that lingered with me after graduation (and for the last [almost] 20 years) was this: It will be an effort—and a privilege—to put yourself out there in the world, to see and experience all that's out there, and to see and recognize when you're onto something special.

That summer, I took on my first professional (and freelance) project in the real-world: writing a Teacher Resource Guide to accompany the production of *Honus and Me* at Pittsburgh's City Theatre.

I had interned at City Theatre between my junior and senior year of college. After several summers working as a day camp counselor, I figured this last summer between college years was the time to get a real internship. My boss at City Theatre, Diane, was the director of education. She was one of the first truly professional women I'd met, yet alone, worked with. I remember my first phone interview with her for the internship role from my dorm room one Friday afternoon. I had pulled in on two wheels from a beer run with friends right before the phone call. Talking with Diane fresh off that errand was a shock into reality. She was serious and professional; I felt like I was neither at the time. How could I be as a 20-year-old English major?

Diane must have sensed something different. She hired me a couple of weeks later for an internship with her education department. At the time, it was a thrilling experience. I loved working with the "behind-the-scenes" administration team at the theater, which was a restored church on Pittsburgh's South Side. I read plays written by nine-year-olds and casually passed then emerging talent, now Tony-award winner, Billy Porter, who was performing in Suzan-Lori Parks' play, *Topdog/Underdog*, which was at City Theatre that year.

Diane brought me back for a short-term contract role a year later, the summer I graduated from college. It was reminiscent of the work I had done the previous summer, except that this time it was for a specific project.

Honus and Me is a children's novel by Dan Gutman that tells the story of a struggling 10-year-old baseball player named Joe who finds a rare 1909 T-206 Honus Wagner baseball card. There are lots of lessons in there, but in a Sandlot-like experience, Joe finds himself meeting and tossing a ball with Wagner, the legendary Pittsburgh Pirate widely considered to be one of the most famous shortstops in baseball history. Playwright Steven

Dietz adapted the book into a play, which played at City Theatre in 2006.

Writing the Teacher Resource Guide could have been a very simple plug-and-play exercise. I very easily could have scanned the Internet for information and snagged pictures from other websites. But, as a recent college grad hungry for that $250 project, I ran with it. I emailed with the Pittsburgh Pirates archivists; I sat in on play rehearsals; I talked to teachers.

Diane and I would piece this 15-page guide together, almost as if we were building a yearbook. Suffice it to say, I got really into it. Twenty years later, it's still one of the professional projects I am the proudest to have produced, for a couple of reasons.

At the time, I was neither a teacher nor a baseball fan, so I needed to find a way into this story. In the scheme of this project, that meant talking to teachers and other people who knew a lot more about baseball than I ever would. It also meant showing up with probably the oddest and most ill-framed or off-the-beaten-path questions from a place of having no idea what I was talking or writing about.

The other piece I latched onto early in the project was that, yes, this was a resource guide designed for teachers bringing students to see the show to teach on the story and its themes. But this was really a people story. The play was about people even if one of them was a very specific historic character, and this guide was designed for people—teachers, students, perhaps even families. It occurred to me that thinking and writing was always about people. I'd never seen it like that before, and I wondered if others did.

As important as that was, it wasn't the biggest lesson I learned that summer. No, that was this thing that happens when we choose to get really into something.

Growing up, our Volvo 240 had a button on the side of the gear shift labelled Overdrive. You'd hit the button when you needed more power, such as merging onto a highway or climbing a hill. I thought of it as a boost when we needed another level of power. This project pushed my own overdrive button.

At the time, I was looking for a job. I didn't have much to do. I was stuck between flipping through pictures from college and trying to figure out my next steps. And yet, out of nowhere, overdrive kicked in. Why? Because I was helping tell a story that had never been told before.

Where does overdrive come from? Maybe from fear; maybe perfectionism; sometimes from a deep need to achieve or impress. In many cases, though, I think what's lying underneath each of those is an innate sense of curiosity. We're curious what could happen if we followed this thread, if we kicked it into gear, if we pushed just one more layer deeper or wider. I'd venture to say the majority of rabbit holes, whether they're real or imagined, are dug up from curiosity that's sparked by an internal overdrive button we've pushed within ourselves.

The funny thing is that we don't necessarily need overdrive— or, at least, some of us don't. I know a lot of people who are completely comfortable never pressing that button. I know others who thrive on overdrive. Though it might not be entirely accurate to say this, I find the people who need overdrive the most are the ones who crave the ability to see 360 degrees of something, whether that's a problem, an opportunity, a story, or *themselves*.

In this case, I needed overdrive because I was desperate for an intellectual challenge. I missed college. I missed the good questions, the deep discussions; and I hate to say it, but I even missed the red ink and feedback from professors, because they were barometers to help me measure achievement and success. I needed overdrive to help me rise to this challenge.

Pushing your own overdrive button is a choice, but when we get really into something, it changes the way we tell the story. This inevitably has the power to change that story for everyone who will consume or digest it. In this case, as in the case of many creative projects, it's a challenge and opportunity to show all 360 degrees of a final product, i.e., to show every angle and side. That's only possible when we do 360 degrees of preparation.

Is overdrive related to passion? It might be. Our culture today is obsessed with the word "passion," i.e., strong, almost uncontrollable emotions or drives. With that said, I think of overdrive as passion with momentum. People always feel the results of that when we put that overdrive level of preparation and passion into something.

The 360 degrees for this project looked different than any other work I had done before. While researching, I discovered that Wagner's grave was in a cemetery 20 minutes from where I lived. Coincidentally, it was also in the same cemetery where three generations of my mother's family were laid to rest.

There are people who find this sort of information and think, "Cool," but do nothing more.

There are people who find this information and think, "Let's go. Let's follow the thread."

I will always be the person who follows the thread.

So, I drove over to the cemetery in Jefferson Hills one warm afternoon, walked into the main office, and asked if someone could help me find Honus Wagner's grave.

They pulled out their cemetery guide and found the plot. Armed with a set of numbers that represents quadrants on a map, I got back into my car and drove to a hillside dotted with thousands of graves. And started walking.

With a headstone lying flush to the ground, there was the grave of one of the greatest baseball players of all time: Honus Wagner, 1874–1955. Yellow flowers decorated the grave.

Did I write about that experience for the Teacher Resource Guide? No. Did I tell anyone about my visit to Wagner's grave? Maybe a handful of people would understand my need to follow the thread. Did I need to do that to complete the project? Absolutely not.

Maybe it was a move to impress a boss, for whom I had so much respect. But really, I think it was simply a move to push the story forward by understanding Wagner not just as a famous ballplayer, but as a human. It allowed me to see all 360 degrees, from where it all started, from whom it all started; to make him real and tangible.

So many times, we see or read stories online—on computers or tablets, scrolling on our phones. But those stories, though rich in words and language, will always be two-dimensional. When we choose to go, to follow the thread, to push the overdrive button, we can turn a two-dimensional story into three-dimensional version, with more angles and better perspectives.

It's harder to pursue three-dimensional stories. It takes effort, time, energy, and attention. Often, it's worth it.

I often think about this when I'm working on projects today; how following a thread might not be necessary, yet, it is. It comes up a lot when I'm meeting new people or hiring—and I wonder what overdrive looks like for them, or even whether they have an overdrive button.

Are there signals that someone has the overdrive button? Yes. It sometimes looks like a person who asks one deeper, more challenging question—not in an obnoxious way, but in a curious way; or it can look like a job candidate who has gone the extra mile before the interview to investigate and research with no guarantee he or she will get the job. They do it because they're curious; they do it because there's a thread to follow.

We're not always rewarded by pushing overdrive. Oftentimes, we're not. We do it because we want to. And we want to because something deeply rooted whispers that we need to explore that curiosity.

There's also sometimes a cost we pay in burnout, mental exhaustion, or intellectual or physical fatigue. Because overdrive isn't a constant state of being. You can't be in overdrive all the time. If you were, you'd be completely drained every day. No, overdrive is something that you use when you need it, and then release, like that button on my family's old Volvo.

There's also real overdrive and fake overdrive. Let me explain. Several years ago, training for marathons and half-marathons was trending among a group of my friends. People would talk about doing these weekend-long road races in the North Carolina mountains, or training for triathlons. I thought it was something I wanted to do.

I started to train for a half-marathon. I hated every moment, but I kept at it, convinced that overdrive would kick in, or if it didn't, I'd figure out a way to push that button. Then, I pulled a groin muscle which meant I couldn't run at all for months. It was a curse—and a blessing. I realized I was faking it the entire time. It took my body shutting down for me to quit trying to force an overdrive that wasn't ever going to happen for someone who is happiest running 3.2 miles—not 12.1 miles.

Sometimes that is simply asking or wondering: What would they do or how far would they go if they didn't know the subject, e.g., if they weren't a teacher or a baseball fan. On a broader scale, it's a question of how far would they go to follow the thread?

prompts for radical change

In case you missed it, this is a conversation about when you kick it into overdrive to pursue your curiosity—and find something cool on the other end. That overdrive can be operational, emotional, personal or professional; and if you think back on it, it probably started early in your life.

- What is your earliest memory of pursuing something while in overdrive mode?
- What's your overdrive look like or feel like now?
- How far do you go to follow the thread(s)?
- When do you let things go, and choose not to pursue them?
- What's a personal or professional project that inspired you to really kick it into gear—why then, why there?

CHAPTER THREE: take ownership

Any amateur golfer will tell you that one of the worst moments in a round of golf is the first tee shot when you're playing with people you've never played with before. You don't know their skill or talent; and they don't know yours. Although there's always some grace given for that first tee shot, you can't ever really fake it. You must own that moment from the second you saddle up to the tee. You can never bullshit or fluff your way through that moment. It's 100% percent yours.

Just a couple of weeks before I started my first year as a high school English teacher, twelfth grade world literature, I was warned that my afternoon class was just, and I'm paraphrasing, "a really interesting mix of characters."

I was 23 years old, new to Charlotte, NC, and new to teaching. I began the school year as the full-time replacement for a teacher who left at the end of the previous school year and who was much older and more experienced than me. I had several weeks to work alongside a colleague, Allison, before she took maternity leave. I arrived several weeks before school started, to get a lesson from her and pick up a binder of materials. In that meeting, she told me that she and colleagues had already seen the roster for that afternoon class.

According to Allison, it was a surly bunch. I'm sure the initial thought was that the previous teacher—older and more experienced—could handle them, but I might not be ready.

I remember Allison saying something along the lines of. "We tried to prevent it for you, but it just can't really be avoided."

Included in the group were several students who were still upset that some of their friends had been kicked out of the same school the year before; there was an aspiring rapper; there was a young and talented racecar driver who, I was told, would need his Blackberry with him.

As a 23-year-old first-time teacher, I didn't have the faintest idea what I was doing, in general. Add in a literal class of characters, and I was a special kind of clueless.

True to advanced billing, they came with an attitude, respectively and collectively. There were 17 in the class—14 men and three women—all high school seniors, living in between worlds of finishing high school and planning for college. Their twelfth grade world literature class was never really anything they got excited about—or even cared about. Assignments were consistently late, papers were turned in with text language instead of real language, which meant I would be correcting the letter "b" by asking that it be spelled out as "be." The side panel of a race car was brought in one day; a glass bottle of Cheerwine soda shattered on the table. They were always up to something. And they didn't let anything slip. If I missed anything, they'd jump on it. I sometimes felt like I was back in high school, yet I was the teacher.

The schedule rotated daily which meant anyone—student or teacher—had to be on their time management game constantly with when-to-be-where. That first year of teaching, I felt like I needed a cheat sheet to stay organized and remember where I needed to be.

It worked, until it didn't.

There was always one block of time each afternoon when I wasn't teaching, and I usually spent it sitting at my computer desk in the teacher's workroom. Typically, I worked through the entire period.

One afternoon, five minutes before the end of the period, two students from the afternoon world literature section came into the teacher's workroom.

"Hey, where were you in class today?" one asked. I was confused, until I saw the other student snicker.

"We have class next," I said.

"No, we had class now," the other said.

My heart started to race. *Shit,* I thought, hustling down the hallway.

When I arrived, most of the students were still sitting in the classroom. But they weren't all there. Some had left to go find food when they realized I wasn't coming to class. Most of them stayed just to hang out. There might have been music playing. I remember it feeling like spring break in there.

They had known I was right down the hall in the teacher's workroom, yet no one came to get me at first. Finally, they sent two students as tributes to break the news to me that I'd messed up—five minutes before class ended.

As the bell signaled that their class period was over, and that my *real* planning period was beginning, I laughed it off with them, even as they mercilessly noted how I messed up the schedule. I was embarrassed, completely aware that wherever they were going next, they'd be announcing that I messed up the schedule and missed my own class.

I sloughed it off with an "oh, well" attitude, mixed with a "will I ever be taken seriously again" angst. As a perfectionist who is constantly kicking herself when I make moves like this, I was fragile—both cool and confused. In my first year teaching high school, I had figured out which battles to pick—and which battles to move on from. There was really nothing I could do about it now... right?

Back in the teacher workroom during my *real* planning time block, I explained the situation to Eileen, an English teacher colleague. Eileen was a much more experienced teacher with decades of the craft under her belt. As I got to the end of the story, she had a different reaction.

"They should have told you," she said. "I think you need to hold them accountable for that."

Eileen's suggestion lingered in my head for hours after that.

She's right, I thought, *I should have held them accountable.* My cool confusion turned into anger—and put me on a quest to prove that they should have told me. It was their fault, not mine.

Later that night, I fired an email off to those students explaining that we'd be discussing it the next day during class. When class rolled around, I came in ready for a fight. I asked each of them to write a short essay on how that experience related to something we'd read during the year. With a reading list that included Shakespeare and Homer, that assignment was a stretch.

As I explained the assignment, I could see their eyes roll. And if I didn't see them, I felt them.

I didn't stop there. I had a whole monologue ready for them: How the way you do one thing is the way you do everything, and choosing not to tell me was not going to be acceptable in college— or the working world. Even though I had just pulled that move in the working world.

I lost more respect by my reaction the next day than the actual day-of behavior itself. This is because my reaction that next day had nothing to do with them. It had everything to do with me. My ego was trying to overcorrect the checkmate they'd called.

Should they have come in and told me I was missing my own class? Probably.

Should I have managed my schedule better? Yes.

Should I have held them accountable? Maybe.

Should I have held myself accountable in front of them? Yes.

There were a couple of lessons here.

My first reaction was my truest reaction. That was me. As cool but confused as I was, I wasn't really going to push it with them; I knew them best, and they knew me pretty well, too.

But we sometimes, oftentimes, let other people get into our heads. In this case, it was Eileen. Although she had the best intentions and an approach that was probably right for her, it wasn't right for me. I ended up delivering a monologue—with a stack of lame essays to grade—all because of my own mistake. I doubt I taught any real lesson that next day—other than solid proof someone told me to do something about it, which was true.

At the end of the day, they were teenagers trying to be cool. Whether they had any debate as to whether to come find me before they actually did, I'll never know.

At the very bottom of that experience, I was desperately trying to distract them from my own mistake; to recover my own ego; to be taken seriously. In trying to correct it—they sniffed it out. They knew it, too. I remember that my voice as I assigned this ridiculous essay didn't even sound like me. They must have guessed that an older, wiser teacher coached me as a remedy—or that I was trying to save face.

I would have made a bigger impression had I just owned my mistake. By not doing so, I missed my own lesson, literally and figuratively.

Over the years, I've seen the same behavior in other people. There's either a lack of responsibility or accountability or a drastic move to right the wrong in a way that's over the top and even inappropriate. It's the recession's fault; it's inflation's fault; it's the sales department's fault; it's creative's fault.

We have a funny expression in my family: When you don't take responsibility for something, we call it passing the blame potato. Just like the childhood game of hot potato, the blame potato is equally hot—just in an entirely different way.

Every single time I've seen it, I know it's a complicated move to try to save face—to not be embarrassed or called out; or, to get ahead of the storm in a way that gaslights or makes someone else feel like they're responsible.

Taking ownership isn't anything new; I've read books about it by Navy SEALs; I've heard professional development workshops discuss it. You can read about it and hear about it all you want, but when you're in the moment, the difference is this: What are you going to do?

There's another side of the *own it* conversation that's especially prevalent in entrepreneurial or business owner conversations, and it's this adage to *fake it 'til you make it.*

I've heard plenty of podcasts, panel discussions, and Instagram reels advising young or early entrepreneurs to act bigger, sound bigger, be bigger. For all intents and purposes, give the world a bit of a show to get them on board with whatever you're building. It works for a while—until it gets exhausting.

Yes, it might work for your first six months, until you start getting clients, start building a reputation, start onto a true path, but I worry about anyone who keeps it going beyond that. Because then, it becomes a lifestyle—and it perpetuates a false narrative.

About ten years ago, a woman named Elizabeth Holmes hit the mainstream media with her blood testing company, Theranos. We all know how that ended up, but ten years ago, she was cool, impressive, and intimidating. Though I've never met her, there's always this comparison thing that happens when you're in the same age bracket as other people. Holmes and I are around the same age, born within six months of each other, so as she gained celebrity, there was a part of me that thought: *I'm not doing enough. Should I be farther along in my career? Did I not try hard enough? Why didn't I think of anything that landed me on Forbes?*

Inevitably, I felt like I should be more. Little did I realize that she was deep into faking it until she made it—with empty promises to investors, products and services that failed, partnerships that she would never be able to fulfill. It's good proof that the fake it 'til you make it approach might make a compelling impression, but it can also do serious damage.

If you want to try that approach, you have to know when to transition to full-on ownership. You will know that shift, but I can guarantee it'll come in a moment where your gut tells you that you need to step up. From that point forward, you can never go back to faking it 'til you make it.

I always say that I learned a bit of my business attitude teaching world literature to high school seniors—specifically, second semester high school seniors. They always saw right through the bullshit—and called me on it.

This isn't a call to action to start naming other people's fluff; it's an opportunity to take ownership of what's yours—the good, the bad, the cool and confusing, the complicated.

Taking ownership isn't about anything other than just taking responsibility for your actions in the least-bullshit way possible.

I've stayed in touch with a handful of students since teaching. They went on to college and careers; now, marriage and families. Recently, fifteen years after that experience, I had dinner with several former students, two of whom were the mercenaries who came into the teacher's workroom that day to tell me I'd missed my own class.

"Hey, do you remember that one time you missed class?" one of two asked me during dinner. The other snickered, yet again.

"Yes, yes, I do."

prompts for radical change

In case you missed it, this is a conversation about taking ownership of your actions. The funny thing about this one is that it applies to the big life *things* – and the daily, unsexy *things*, too. It's about calling out or owning your own fluff.

- How do you define "ownership"?
- Is it the same definition for your personal life as it is for your professional life?
- When have you chosen not to take ownership?
- How'd that experience feel—and what happened?
- When you do choose to own it, how does it feel?

CHAPTER FOUR:
find what innovation
means to you

When I was in fifth grade, all I wanted to do was play basketball. Like many kids who grew up in the early '90s, that love started with Michael Jordan. Growing up in in Chicago meant that every kid knew who Michael Jordan was. He was the epitome of cool—as both a human being and a basketball player. Unless you were one of the soccer kids who loved Pelé, Michael Jordan was one of the first brands we fell in love with as kids growing up in that era. He was the first cardboard cutout that kids stood up as a fixture in their rooms, 24/7 inspiration. Without even knowing it, he was convincing kids— both boys and girls— to play basketball.

I was one of those kids. I loved Michael Jordan. So much so that I gave out Michael Jordan Valentines one February 14. My natural next move was to play.

But our elementary school didn't have a team. And I didn't know any girls who played basketball. Two years before then, we had moved to Plano, Tex., so as an elementary school kid, I was unsure how to find a team of fifth grade girls who had an opening for a new player like me—where do you go? The local YMCA? Our suburb's recreation department?

What felt easier at the time was starting something from nothing.

It seemed completely logical to me at the time that if something didn't exist, we needed to create it. Though I had a handful of friends, I didn't know if anyone liked the idea of basketball or even wanted to play. So I took it upon myself. I needed to start it.

I went to my parents with my idea: I wanted to start a basketball team.

My dad replied, "If you find ten girls, I'll coach."

Though I don't remember my exact reaction, I imagine being ten years old and hearing that was annoying. How was I supposed to do that?

And yet, it felt reasonable. There could be no team without players. We needed to build a team with people. No one else was going to do it unless I did it.

A sense of old soul logic kicked in once again—*Well. Okay. Let me try and see what happens.*

I'll start asking around.

I built a list of girls who I knew liked sports, who excelled at things like recess. I also added alternates, i.e., the girls I thought might be convinced.

As an adult, I understand why my father said that. He was trying to see how badly I wanted it. He wasn't going to commit to anything until I put all my cards on the table. If I was really that committed, I'd find the team; if it was a fleeting idea, he'd never hear about it again. In that sense, an offer to coach ten, fifth grade girls a new sport, for a daughter who just really liked Michael Jordan, was unlikely to manifest into a commitment.

A couple of weeks later, I came to him with a list of ten girls who wanted to play basketball. I had campaigned, which meant recruiting ten girls during lunch or recess or by calling their home phones after school. And I found them. All we needed were their parents' signatures. We drove around in a couple of days to get all those signatures. All ten girls—and all their parents—agreed. In just a couple of weeks, the Brinker Teddies (named for the Brinker Elementary School's Teddy bear mascot) was born.

It was a team that hadn't ever existed until that moment.

Twenty years later, I'd do the same thing, but this time, with a company—and a career.

My first semester at business school was absolutely miserable. I was failing two of the three classes—constantly lost in accounting and statistics content. Even worse, I had psyched myself out. I had convinced myself the first week that I didn't belong in business school. Everyone was strong at the subjects I was taking for the very first time; everyone knew how to work Excel; everyone knew what they were doing. I was lucky—maybe even happy—if I got a C on an assignment, because I was getting Cs and Ds across a variety of assignments in accounting and statistics.

One of the business program managers called me when I was at the mall just days before Christmas. She was calling to tell me that I was on academic probation for the spring semester, starting in January. A life-long perfectionist who had probably scored a half a dozen Cs across my entire academic career was now drowning in them. If I could have lit a cigarette outside the **lululemon** store, I probably would have.

This wasn't me. For a split second, I thought about quitting the program. Maybe this wasn't my path. But I also remember my mom giving me a pep talk to remind me: I wasn't a quitter.

I wallowed in disappointment over the Christmas holidays but then realized my mom was right. I wasn't a quitter.

That old school logic kicked in again: *Well. Okay. Let's see what happens.*

That second semester, the game changed because I changed the way I approached it. Granted, I was in more comfortable classes for me—leadership and organizational studies—but I also started to see my way in. I started to see the things that came naturally to me—in this case, people, leadership, and teams—didn't always come naturally to those who were good at accounting and statistics. Granted, that's a generalization, but it helped me to see my "in."

I also saw an opportunity.

Many times, I'd see classmates use numbers to sell a theory or an idea. They'd pop a pivot table up and talk us all through it. It felt logical. It felt like what you'd do if you were in business school.

But there was something else I was craving. Where were the people in these talks? Where was the soul and personality and warmth and story behind the numbers, the theory, the idea?

I wanted to know *why* these presenters wanted to start this business.

Where *was* humanity and the creativity behind the reason we do business in the first place?

I found myself wanting to know the story, the why, the people involved, the vision. There had to be a place to focus on that in business, right?

Traditionally, you'd go to an agency to do this work—one of those sexy, smooth advertising or marketing firms that so many English majors head to after undergrad. I interviewed at one right out of college. I walked in, and I fell in love with the office, the people, the art on the walls. It felt cool and creative. Until I sat down with the creative director who told me she had no idea why I was there. I had no agency experience. I hadn't interned anywhere that would set me up well for a job there. My degree from Kenyon didn't really matter. For all intents and purposes, she schooled me. At 21 years old, unemployed and trying to find a job, I rode the train home from downtown Pittsburgh crying.

Since that day, I felt PTSD every time I thought about interviewing at an agency. Ten years later, I still didn't have agency experience—even though I had several other professional experiences.

Much like that fifth grade basketball team, **toth shop** was born from this idea that what I wanted to do didn't yet exist—a place to be both a businessperson and creative thinker, that looked different than a marketing department or an advertising agency, that got to rewrite the traditional marketing rules a bit with a niche that focused on really good thinking and writing, specifically.

I wanted it to be a place that had my touch.

Why do people like me make moves like that? Is it to be contrarian or difficult? Maybe. Maybe it's just because, at the end of the day, we can. There are a lot of times something doesn't fit into a box that's already been built. So, we build a new box—a new team, a new concept or company.

If you're naturally drawn to this kind of approach, you're probably also fascinated by the question of what's possible.

I remember when I started to think about the idea of **toth shop**, I said to myself: *I don't want to get to 40 years old and wonder what it could have been.*

I wasn't willing to risk not trying.

I wouldn't start **toth shop** for another two years after that—after my first freelance client asked me if I'd ever consider taking what I was doing for her on a very part-time basis, full time.

Though I'd considered it loosely, I started to think about it more seriously after that conversation.

Which is another lesson: Yes, there's the idea and the concept we float around in our own heads, but it also often takes a nudge from someone else to get it moving.

In the case of the Teddies, it was the challenge to find ten, fifth grade girls to form a team.

In the case of **toth shop**, it was one question posed by someone other than me, who saw a vision for it, too.

As much as we talk about innovation, there's a level of innovation that needs to happen first. It's internal; it's personal. It's that moment you realize you want something that doesn't yet exist out there. It's that voice inside that says, *Well. Okay. Let's try it.*

No one will ever tell you this, but that voice is actually the most innovative part of the process.

Yes, innovation is the doing of things, the making of widgets.

It's also the thinking that gets you from no basketball team existing to ten girls on a team; from a failing business school experience to finding the right lane—and speaking at the MBA graduation ceremony—to starting your own agency, with your own rules.

prompts for radical change

In case you missed it, this is about how you choose to innovate and transform your life. When you make moves like that, it impacts both your personal and professional life.

- Consider who's (or what's) nudged you recently?
- How, when, or where did you feel the nudge—and did you do anything about it?
- What's the idea that keeps coming back, and why?
- When have you ignored the nudge—what happened?
- What was the fifth grade basketball story that has become a thread for your life?

CHAPTER FIVE:
define agility

Locals call it the "Dead Zoo." I'm talking about the Natural History Museum, a branch of the National Museum of Ireland on Merrion Street in Dublin. Built in 1856, neither the building nor the collection have changed much since then. There's a quiet mustiness to the building that feels both familiar and otherworldly.

That sense of otherworldliness might also be because of the collection itself. That collection is over two million items that are a biologist-zoologist dream—everything from insects to giant Irish deer (sometimes called the "Irish elk"). If you're wondering how that's possible, the insects' wings are pinned down; the giant Irish deer are stuffed. This is, in fact, a zoo of animals that are a long time dead and a long time stuffed. A dead zoo.

My sister, Maret, and I originally had no intention of going here while in Dublin in August 2019.

But, on a post-rain, sunny Thursday morning, the *Book of Kells* in the Old Library at Trinity College was opening at noon versus their usual 8:30am, which threw a slight monkey wrench into our morning agenda. So, we made a quick decision; we grabbed hot teas to-go from Brewley's and made the 15-minute walk to the museum. Days before, a Wicklow resident with a British accent referred to it as the "stuffed animal museum." Our expectations floated somewhere between low and high—and befuddlement as to what this place really was.

We were the first two visitors that morning. Admission is free, so we wandered first through the sleepy ground floor Irish Room, complete with a giant, stuffed Irish deer that I never even knew existed, as well as dozens of mounted birds and fish native to or found in Ireland. We looked up to see a basking shark hanging from the ceiling.

We then crept up the stairs to the first floor. As the first humans in this space on this day, we yanked open the door and stepped onto a creaky wooden floor into a two-story room with a vaulted ceiling made of glass, much like an old train station. We were then greeted by hundreds of dead, stuffed animals— everything from buffalos to tigers, polar bears to elephants. The room was dead silent; spooky and beautiful; goosebump-worthy and awe-inspiring; peculiar and yet, natural.

I made my way through the room, wandering through rows of stuffed animals, looking at each one individually. As soon as I got to the opposite side, I looked back to see the whole collection— some of which are now endangered and extinct animals; some of which still are natural predators. And in a weird *Night at the Museum* moment, I thought to myself: *If in this moment, everything in this room came alive, who would survive? The biggest, the strongest, the smartest, the most aggressive? The polar bear, the gorilla, the lion? Who's making it out of this room?* Standing among those hundreds of stuffed animals, I didn't have an easy answer.

People think like that a lot today. *Everything* has *everything* to do with who's the fastest, biggest, strongest, fiercest, most aggressive, smartest, loudest.

As we walked out, thanking the staff, I did a double take to read a Darwin quote painted on the wall.

"It is not the most intellectual of the species that survives; it is not the strongest that survives; but the species that survives is the one that is able to adapt to and to adjust best to the changing environment in which it finds itself."

Survival has nothing to do with being the fastest, biggest, strongest, smartest, or loudest.

It's the one who sees change coming, who feels a stirring in the wind, who listens to the world around her, and adapts, adjusts, grows, evolves, and transforms. It's the one who practices fluidity in the face of fear.

In today's business world, "agility"—or the ability to move quickly and easily—gets confused with "flexibility," maybe even "adaptability." They're both similar and different. "Flexibility" and "adaptability" speak to fluidity and the natural ability to change shapes and forms. It's where we get that feeling that we need to "just roll with it" or "go with the flow." That's all true—in the right context. Agility does that, too, while also challenging us to keep a certain pace. This means that agility includes both fluidity and pace.

In 2012, my mom was diagnosed with triple negative breast cancer. This unexpected news devastated our family, which had no known history of breast cancer. On the day we received the official diagnosis, I drove out to my parents' house. After a lot more tears, Mom turned to me in the Adirondack chair on the back porch and said, "Whatever this is, we have to be aggressive and available."

Aggressive in the treatments—available for whatever was going to go up through the process.

Maybe that's what agility is today. Maybe agility is showing up with strength and flexibility—being aggressive and available. In Mom's case, it took approximately six months of a variety of treatments—including a lumpectomy, radiation, and chemotherapy—to cure the cancer. Ten years later, she remains cancer-free.

It's that pace that makes a difference. Mind you, pace is not speed, not momentum. So, now if I ask, *who's making it out of that room*? I know the answer. The most agile one.

The world practiced agility through the 2020 COVID-19 pandemic. It hit home for **toth shop**, as well. By the start of 2020, the micro-agency that started as a part-time, side-hustle shop managing social media for a handful of clients was on the brink of major change.

To meet clients where they were, i.e., unsure how to talk about who they were or how they were managing the pandemic from a product and service perspective—we leaned into the need. We shifted services and packages to meet customers where they were. We immersed ourselves in more project work versus long-term client work. This included projects like rewriting websites for clients or helping them launch new ideas, versus trying to sell them monthly retainers.

Don't get me wrong, we fought our way through 2020 and 2021. It was a total shift in how we chose to serve people. Yet, 2020 served as a springboard for growth, because we chose to take an informed risk to be fluid and flexible, to be aggressive and available, to practice agility in ways we had never done before.

In case you were wondering, the giant, Irish elk taxidermized in the Dead Zoo's lobby went extinct some 8,000 years ago as the Earth started to warm. In Ireland, as glaciers melted, lakes formed, and the antlers and bodies of the Irish elk fell into the lakes and sank into sediment at the bottom of the lake. Over time, they were covered with peat, preserving them until they were rediscovered and displayed in Ireland's oldest museum. It proves an excellent point about survival: You're born during a certain time in history, but the scenery and circumstances may vary. The fight for survival by a giant mammal 8,000 years ago looked a lot different than ours does today.

prompts for radical change

In case you missed it, this is a conversation about agility, i.e., your personal and professional ability to move, act, and think quickly.

- How would you define your own agility?
- When, how, or where are you most agile?
- What's possible when we choose to practice agility?
- Who or what taught you agility?
- Who do you teach or model agility to?

CHAPTER SIX:
figure out how you process curveballs

The Hofburg was not what I thought it would be at all.

When I read that it was built in the 13th century as the primary imperial palace of the Habsburg dynasty, my American brain immediately went to "castle," and down a rabbit hole of everything movies and televisions have told us a castle would be: rolling countryside, maybe a vineyard, a grand entrance, stained glass windows, flanking towers, postern gates... maybe a moat. A palace would have a moat, right?

As I stood in front of the Hofburg, in the heart of Vienna, Austria, on a bitterly cold November morning, reality was pretty far off from my preconceptions. The Hofburg is a regal palace, but different than I'd ever imagined; it feels tall and organized and angular, like a place where you would do business and politics rather than a place to live.

I was there for the first time in November 2018, as a guest of the Peter Drucker Forum and, more specifically, as one of the winners of the Peter Drucker Challenge.

The Peter Drucker Forum is an annual event held for business thought leaders from around the world. It's organized for modern thinking, with inspiration from Peter Drucker, one of the great minds of management thinking. Drucker is often quoted by people who understand that business is, more often than not, another expression of the humanities.

The Peter Drucker Challenge is a writing competition for students and managers under the age of 35. The competition releases a theme each year with writing prompts for writers around the world to address in essays. The goal for participants is to land within the top ten for your appropriate category because, as a top ten winner, you're invited to Vienna for the Forum, and to receive an award.

The first time I entered the Challenge, I was in my last semester of business school. I spent hours shaping and reshaping that essay. It felt like something you'd submit to a business school professor. I submitted it to their editorial review committee and waited. I received word several months later that I landed somewhere between 11 and 15—but not the top ten.

I gave up submitting to the contest for four years, until I got the itch to try it again. That particular year's theme was The Rise of Artificial Intelligence. I had half-baked thoughts about AI, but nothing serious. I rattled ideas around for weeks and months, but I felt like I couldn't come up with a good start, until I went on a date with a guy who was going on and on about how he was using AI for customer service.

"So, they don't talk to a human, they talk to a computer," I asked him over a half-priced glass of happy hour wine.

"Yes," he answered.

That works if you're a large corporation, I guess, but this guy owned a hyper-local brewery. It felt ridiculous that a customer taking the time to call couldn't talk to a real person. That just didn't sit right with me.

In that moment, I found the opening to my essay. I wrote my Challenge essay in one sitting—on a Sunday morning two days before the deadline—and I submitted it with no revision. I wrote it with my perspective and in my voice, with a little edge and spice. After my previous 11th to 15th place submission, I had nothing to lose in trying an entirely different approach.

A couple of weeks later, I received an email: I landed within the top ten for the managers category, and the Peter Drucker Forum was inviting me to Vienna for the event and the ceremony, fully paid for by the Forum. I was going to Vienna!

A few weeks later, I went to the Challenge's website to learn that I had earned a third-place finish for my category. I could hardly believe it. I had listened to my gut feeling to try again, and I did it my way—and landed in the top three.

In the weeks before I traveled to Vienna, every imposter syndrome thought came to my mind. I waited to buy a dress for the ceremony because I didn't really think I earned it; I kept asking *Why me?*

I re-read my essay, and I found some mistakes. It was like picking a scab—I was trying to find something wrong.

Several days before I was to fly to Vienna, I received an email from someone on the editorial committee asking me if I'd like to be a panel member for the event's closing presentation. Having seen pictures from previous events, I knew this meant standing or sitting on an elevated stage, in a ballroom, with an audience of around 1,000 people. That gut voice returned—*say yes*.

I said "yes" and, of course, unraveled in imposter syndrome before boarding the plane and making my way from Charlotte to Munich to Vienna.

In the midst of those doubts, standing alone at the Hofburg, the location of the 2019 Peter Drucker Forum, I felt so small in the scheme of this place and its history.

The two-day Global Peter Drucker Forum reminded me of my college days. When I walked into the Hofburg, I was there for a conference and to accept a third-place writing award. That first morning, the Hofburg was buzzing with thought leaders from around the world, including some whose names I recognized from business school or bookshelves. If you can fan-girl at a business conference, I was deep in the middle. Whether it was the grand and royal location or the brainy, international company, I felt really small in the middle of such a big space and big people, not to mention that me standing there was just one small moment in time for a place nearing seven centuries old.

The event featured panels and breakout sessions with smart conversations, thoughtful insights, and people who worked for places like Harvard or the *Financial Times*.

A writer for the *Financial Times* moderated the panel discussion I sat on. We met briefly, and I asked what to prepare for the session. I don't remember exactly what he said, but I remember thinking: *I'll just be ready for his questions.*

The day of the Final Fireworks panel was a bit of a blur. I would be up there on that stage, sharing thoughts with some of the smartest people I'd ever met. *Why me,* I thought for the one-millionth time. *I can't do this.* At one point, I saw the panel moderator, the writer for the *Financial Times*, in a row ahead of me, scrolling my company's website, most likely finding my career story or notes about my work. Instead of feeling like a badass, I wanted to crawl in a hole. *Just take me off this panel.*

The time came for the panel, and I was asked to report to a specific location to get mic'ed up. At that time, I met the other guests on the panel: Two dinosaurs from another era, and a guy who looked a couple of years older than me. I had read an article about him before I got to Vienna—he had just won a prize to pursue a book concept. He looked smart and scholarly, but also kind of like he was on his own planet, as if he'd just cracked cold fusion but wasn't sure whom to tell.

"Are you ready for this panel?" he asked, as the assistant looped a microphone cable around his body.

"Oh, for sure," I said.

"What are you going to say for your three minutes?"

"My three minutes?" I asked.

"Yeah, we each get three minutes to share general thoughts," he answered.

The room was starting to spin. An assistant came over to clip a mic on my collar. We were five minutes away from this panel and every fear I had—from the weeks leading up to the event until now—were becoming real.

Shit.

I was ready to answer questions, but I was not prepared to talk on anything for three minutes. I was in full-on panic mode. In this context, three minutes might as well be 25 years. Have you ever talked about something for three minutes straight? I mean, three minutes on *what*?

If you can imagine my imposter syndrome before this moment, you can imagine what it was like now. I was hit by an avalanche of every doubt I could imagine: *Why wasn't I prepared? Why didn't I ask more questions? Why didn't I have three minutes of something prepared even though I didn't realize that was going to be a thing I needed to do? Why didn't I see that coming?*

As you can imagine, some of those thoughts were completely made up by the gremlins we all have in our heads. Still, these questions didn't stay in my head. They swirled through my entire body while I continued to have a conversation with this guy and mingle with others.

I don't want to say that I created this panicked moment, that weeks of imposter syndrome rolling around in my head had somehow manifested in this panic. I don't think the world works like that. But I will say that my body and mind were preparing me for something. I needed a little fear to stay realistic about this opportunity. Someone wiser might make this a moment about why it's important to stay rooted and humble, but what I would do remained to be seen. By one thousand people.

I got up on that stage and took my seat. I was third in line, with the guy who warned me to my left. He was at the end of the line, the last to respond. I remember thinking I should have pushed to have him sit in my seat, but I also had another thought: *I don't want to be the woman on the end.* So, I took the third seat.

The panel's moderator started with a general question that everyone had three minutes to answer. Panelist one spoke. Panelist two started. I was floating between worlds, thinking about what I'd say and listening to them. I can't remember the specifics of what either of them said. I only remember thinking, *we need some chutzpah in here.*

I was bored; it felt old and stale. What could I do? It was right in that second that I remembered Teddy Roosevelt's famous *The Man in the Arena* speech. I'd start there—and figure out the rest along the way.

And that's what I did. I started by citing that speech.

The theatre world has an expression—The White Room—that refers to the feeling of forgetting lines or blanking out on stage. I experienced The White Room for the rest of my time on that panel. I kept talking, I sounded intelligent, I said good things; I just don't remember what they were. To this day, I'm convinced that whatever that gut voice was that got me there, it also got me through those three minutes and the rest of that panel.

I'm not sure that I changed anyone else's life with anything I said, but I changed my own.

It changed the second I took that third seat. Because, in the midst of big anxiety and big imposter syndrome and the big fear that my panic was now causing a sweaty brow and sweaty bangs and an overall look of panic, I had to push forward

I had to for a couple of reasons: One was for women. I needed to prove that in a place so dominated by male leaders there was a seat at the table—or the panel—for me, and I was going to take it. And two: Because when life and work throw you curveballs, you still have to be ready to take a swing.

Being ready for curveballs is one of the oldest tricks in the business book, but at the end of the day, how ready are you for them? Do you take them on despite panic, fear, or anxiety; or do you shrink away? Whatever you choose to do, it's a small moment with a big impact.

Curveballs can be complicated and overwhelming. They can also be good.

Back in 2012, as part of the Democratic National Convention in Charlotte, I was on a team with **lululemon** who was supporting *The Huffington Post's* Oasis. The Oasis was designed to be one central location where stakeholders, politicians, and voting members could retreat for a massage, yoga flow, or just to charge their phones. **lululemon** employees were onsite as support. I felt like a bit of a fish out of water. I wasn't a democrat, so part of me felt a bit out of place. That said, it was also one of the first opportunities when I realized that all I needed to do was just be present as a human—regardless of political affiliation. At one point, Arianna Huffington came into the oasis to moderate a panel with Marcus Samuelsson, the chef and author. She was a pro in her presence and delivery, including how she moved around the room and talked to people.

At one point, she approached two of us and asked about our roles at the Oasis; we told her how we were supporting, and she was appreciative. She also posed for a picture with us. I remember telling her that I'm not a democrat, and I appreciated the opportunity to be a part of this event.

"You should write about that," she said, before being whisked away.

It was another curveball—the good kind. *Arianna Huffington, the person behind the famed Huffington Post, told me I should write about it.*

What does someone do with a curveball like that? You take your best swing.

So, I did. I wrote a 650-word blog about the experience of volunteering for an event for a party and philosophy different from mine, and I submitted it to *The Huffington Post* with a note somewhere along the lines of: "I met Arianna Huffington, and she told me to write about this, and I did."

They published the piece within days—and gave me access to write a column on the website. Over the course of several years, I did. Most notably, I wrote a series about how our family managed an unexpected curveball—my mother's breast cancer diagnosis and treatment. To this day, almost a decade later, those pieces still get readers, and I sometimes hear from a twentysomething or thirtysomething woman whose mother also had breast cancer. In this sense, surviving a curveball becomes part of the flow, i.e., helping others manage their respective curveballs.

The magic here is how you choose to deal with curveballs, because how you choose to deal with them can set you apart from the vast majority of people, many of whom will shrink away or let it pass, because they're uncomfortable. We've heard it a million times: There's something special on the other side of discomfort – it's just a question as to whether you're ready to go there or not.

When faced with the opportunity, just pick up the curveball and do something with it.

prompts for radical change

In case you missed it, this is about what you choose to do with curveballs—whether they're good or challenging—and how you keep moving forward.

- How do you manage those curveball moments fraught with panic and fear?
- How do you manage those curveball moments fraught with potential and opportunity?
- Are your approaches the same or different?
- What's one good move you've made to manage a curveball?

CHAPTER SEVEN:
know the difference
between "I" and "We"

The summer before my senior year of college, while interning at City Theatre, I also interned at *Mister Rogers' Neighborhood*. Fred Rogers had passed away the year before, and the legendary show had been in reruns for years. *The Neighborhood*—managed by Family Communications, Inc., at the time—was working on a series of special projects but, for the most part, maintaining a low profile after decades of not simply production but international fame and success.

How that summer internship came about is a testament to both my own, and *The Neighborhood's,* quirky characters. My mom gave me a book of advice by Mr. Rogers the previous Christmas. Having devoured the show as a kid, I devoured the book in one sitting. And I got to thinking about what they—as in the show's writers, producers, staff—were up to now.

Their offices were located at WQED Pittsburgh, maybe 25 minutes from where we lived. I looked at their website, but there was no indication as to whether they offered summer intern positions. So, I wrote them a letter asking if there were internship opportunities. A couple of weeks later, I received an email from their office. While home for spring break, I found myself in their office waiting room, staring at an enclosed case full of Emmy statutes. I met with David Newell, their director of public relations, who also played the show's mailman, Mr. McFeely. They hadn't had an intern in a while but they were interested in working with me.

I didn't care about a paycheck. Being there wasn't really about anything other than learning from and absorbing what this team produced for generations of children. I started when I returned home for summer break in June.

As plentiful as the boxes and boxes of memorabilia were, so too were the plentiful friends of the show. It was a revolving door of *Mister Rogers' Neighborhood* celebrities who would visit the office. Mr. Rogers' widow, Joanne Rogers, was among them. I was in awe almost every day that I was there. Yet, as joyful as these reunions were, there was also a dark, sacred and magical office there, in the corner. It had belonged to Fred Rogers, and it hadn't been touched since he'd left for the last time. I've never been in a room so quiet yet pulsing with imagination and memory.

I spent most of my time there that summer sorting through and organizing photographs and memorabilia—show notes, fan letters, and fliers from appearances made by Mr. McFeely and the purple panda. It wasn't until a couple of weeks later that I realized a piece of scrap paper with Mr. Rogers' handwriting on it had fallen into my handbag. It was a note either to himself or an assistant about how to respond to a particular fan letter, which I hadn't seen or read.

"Sometimes all we can do is to accept others as they are and 'know' that traditions change through generations. This family is living proof of that."

Twenty years later, I still think about this quote written by Mr. Rogers. I'll never know the context, but I think it has a lot to do with how we show up to work or how we choose to do business.

It would have been so simple for him to write "I" into that sentence, as in, "Sometimes all I can do is to accept others as they are..."

But he didn't write "I," he wrote "we."

It's classic Mr. Rogers, yes, but also a move to get all of us thinking more about "we" versus "I." What can we accept and what can we not accept? What are we capable of? What can we create?

This comes up a lot with clients today—and websites specifically. Clients are feverish to share everything they do, they make, they have. Though it's a company, business, or brand it's a giant "I" in their marketing. It's nothing new, but we're constantly reminding people that, ironically enough, their website isn't about them—it's about the reader. It's about the larger "we."

Also, if we're aware of anything in life and in business, it's this: Things change. Things change all the time. But there are anchors in life that stay the same. We most likely refer to those anchors as "the way it is," or habits or customs or traditions. And it's okay when the traditions change, too. Traditions change because people change—they change through generations, through cultural shifts, through personality shifts. And that's okay.

He also begs a question that I've never been able to shake—across jobs, relationships, personal and professional epiphanies—and it's this: *What are we each living proof of?*

Given the fact this scrap of paper is just that—a scrap of paper—I have no context for the situation to which he was referring. But regardless, it makes me ask, *What is our life, our story, or our legacy a testament to?*

These two sentences are so small yet so mighty. Mighty philosophically in and of themselves, but also mighty in how we choose to use those sentences to look at our brands, our businesses, and our legacies.

Which begs a larger conversation: how to choose to manage and mind our language. If you're stuck thinking I've lost the drive to break down and dissect these one or two sentences like you'd diagram a sentence in fifth grade, you're probably right. But really this is a call to be precise, aware, and mindful of how important even two sentences can be. How they can mean so much more—how they can linger, even out of context, for a good 20 years.

prompts for radical change

In case you missed it, this is a conversation about the "I" versus "we" in your life and what impact means to you.

- How often do you use "we" versus "I"?
- How often does your team use "we" versus "I"? Or pockets of people on your team? (Side note: Why are there even pockets of people who use "we"?)
- What's your business or your work living proof of?
- What traditions do you want to stay the same, and what traditions need to change?
- What are you and/or your family or your community living proof of?

CHAPTER EIGHT:
bring creativity to
unexpected spaces

At the corner of a busy intersection in Bethel Park, Pennsylvania, a suburb 20 minutes outside of downtown Pittsburgh, is St. John the Baptist Byzantine Catholic Cemetery. This Eastern Catholic cemetery is quiet and sleepy—despite how close it sits to a busy traffic stop.

There are hundreds of gravestones that look like you would expect—aged stone and bunches of flowers in various stages of life or death. But, as you look across the hillside, you see one grave that's different than the rest: Andy Warhol.

Since Warhol's passing in 1982, his grave—nestled close to those of his parents—has become a shrine to the creative. There are Campbell's soup cans lining the top of the headstone, pinwheels, and layers of original artwork that've seen many seasons, over many years. As you stand there, it takes time to process the generations of creativity that have taken up residence here, in this most unlikely (but yet, likely) of spots. There's even an opportunity to share your own message to Andy—that you scribble with a marker and leave in a Ziploc bag, fastened down so as not to blow away or be damaged by rain or snow. One woman, Madelyn, collects them all and save them.

It's fitting for the man and his memorial, because it's one of the most creative choices you could make for a cemetery. And it's clear it's been like that for over 30 years—with generations and layers of artists and artwork living with him in this space.

Whoever started that knew they needed to make a move that would honor his legacy—and, in this case, it absolutely had to be a creative choice. It would have been very simple to keep the stoicism and reverence of the generations who passed before him and were also laid to rest in this space. But, someone made a different choice.

Creative choices are both the easiest and hardest decision you'll ever make. Because they depend on how you've been taught to navigate the world—what opportunities or space you've been taught to see in certain moments.

The funniest and smallest moments—or spaces—can become an opportunity for a creative choice.

Before absolutely every quiz or test in my seventh grade Texas history class, our teacher, Ms. Burnham, followed a routine. She passed out the quizzes or tests, then recited this poem:

> The time has come, the walrus said,
> to talk of many things:
> of shoes — and ships — and sealing-wax —
> of cabbages — and kings —
> and why the sea is boiling hot —
> and whether pigs have wings.

She then wished us luck.

As a refresher for those who passed on taking a class in 19th century British lit, that particular passage is an excerpt from Lewis Carroll's poem "The Walrus and the Carpenter."

That poem became so much a part of my life that school year, that I can still recite it verbatim, 30 years later.

In moments of seventh grade anguish and fear looming before multiple choice questions about

Stephen F. Austin or the history of the chuck wagon, she rooted us in both custom and imagination—in a very small space between passing out a test and taking it.

As an adult—and a former high school teacher—I've come to realize just how special that was. Ms. Burnham could have very easily just passed out the tests and returned to her desk. She chose a more creative way.

It was 13 seconds of poetry when you least expected it. It was a really creative choice.

There are opportunities to make creative choices at all times, in all circumstances.

I'll be the first to tell you that creative choices were damn hard in 2020. It was hard to find magic during a global pandemic, cultural and political unrest, and the ever-changing faces of business, work, home, and relationships. Sometimes creativity in 2020 meant just making it through a day without totally losing it.

If I've learned anything about creative choices since then, the major lesson is this: They're hard because they require space— brain space, heart space, soul space. Not a lot of space—just a little. That space was hard to come by in 2020, and it can be hard in other seasons of life. Seasons when there's stress, fatigue, pressure, drama; seasons marked by times when the brain and heart space is limited real estate.

I typically get a lot of ideas and inspiration and energy when I'm out in the world. Like a lot of humans during 2020, I desperately craved travel when I couldn't do it. As a result, I felt idea-less. There were moments when my imagination was like oatmeal you made and forgot on the kitchen counter for hours.

What I've come to realize though is that the travel I so desperately craved (and still do...) is really about creating space— in my brain, heart, and soul—and then filling it. When I realized that, I knew that even just five minutes of space somewhere—on a walk, after a string of Zoom calls, in the car, parked and sitting, was enough to get the creative juices flowing again.

Through the magic of Facebook last year, I asked Ms. Burnham (now Mrs. Johnson) how and why she made that creative choice.

"I read the book *Harriet the Spy* by Louise Fitzhugh the summer before my sixth grade year.

Harriet's nanny Ole Golly used to say that poem when something monumental was happening.

As a teen, I read *Alice in Wonderland*, and the sequel, *Through the Looking Glass*. As you know, it is the eleventh stanza of a poem by Lewis Carroll called 'The Walrus and the Carpenter.' In the fall of 1993 when I began my time at Renner Middle School, I was handing out quizzes in my Texas history class during the first period, and it popped into my memory.

"Ever since then, it has been used in my class. I now say it on the last day of school, and there are certain classes who have to finish the quote for me because my eyes and throat are too clogged with tears."

It's all good proof that making creative choices always needs just a little bit of space.

In that moment, Ms. Burnham made a creative choice—a choice to use poetry to center and focus a class of 13-year-olds, a choice to create a tradition within her classroom that would signal the start of something big—such as a test or quiz. Students felt and experienced that creative choice differently—it became something to center and calm us.

On a whole other level, it was a creative choice that impacted each of us. In that moment and perhaps, as with me, for years to come. To this day, I often think about what I can do in spaces like this to give listeners or students something different or unexpected.

Several years ago, while teaching a career course for a local university, I was trying to think of something fun and different to kick off the first day of school. Typically, students expect a run through of course materials and the syllabus—all materials they were old enough and mature enough to read themselves. What would be different?

So, in that space—that first day of school—I set up several stations around the classroom, and there was one thing at each station: the ingredients and supplies to make slime. When class began that day, I issued them a challenge. They had to form a team and figure out how to make slime—and make it. When I issued the challenge, everyone sat there for a second, baffled that we weren't going to go through the syllabus together.

Some students slowly activated, and then the rest followed. They searched for recipes and instructions online, so they knew what to do with these ingredients. They figured it out and, within 20 minutes, five teams had made slime—and not made a total mess. As always, one student piped in at the end: "What was the point of this activity?"

The point was this: For them to figure out who they were on a team when faced with a challenge. Were they the leader or the follower, the doer or the reader? And then, how did that apply to how they show up in their schoolwork—and perhaps, their careers to come.

In business, we're taught to keep going and moving, to make decisions that honor an overarching goal or bottom line. And that's an important and significant piece of being in business and contributing to impact.

But in those moments, there are opportunities to pause and be creative. I'm not suggesting that every board of directors meeting becomes an art class or a session to talk about feelings or books. But perhaps there's an opportunity there to recenter and reimagine, which is really, truly what creativity is all about.

This isn't about being weird and trying to over-act your way into proving that there's a great difference between art and business; it actually has nothing to do with that. This is about what you choose to do with space—physical space, emotional space, or operational/logistical space? And how you give yourself space to be creative.

When we allow ourselves to step outside of the ordinary, to explore that space, to make a creative choice, we allow ourselves to see what else is possible.

prompts for radical change

In case you missed it, this is about what you choose to do with space—and how you might use it creatively either to recenter, refocus, or perhaps give the world a different way to see space.

- What's the last creative choice you made in a moment that probably didn't require it or that culture told you it'd be weird to do?
- What holds you back from making creative choices?
- What's a creative choice you watched someone else make – what was their reaction to their creative choice?
- What's the most creative *space* you can think of that had or has an impression on you?
- What's been your favorite creative choice you've ever made—big or small, personal or professional?

CHAPTER NINE:
listen between the lines

One of my favorite mentors, Leighton Ford—who has spent 30 years mentoring younger evangelists, pastors, and ministry leaders—opened up his newsletter one week with a good question: "We all know great speakers. How many great listeners do we know?"

How many great listeners do you know? Are you one of them?

I don't think I truly appreciated the importance of listening until I started to teach. When I started to teach, I was really concerned with being heard. I organized lessons to almost the minute with exactly what I would say when. If anything threw me off, I didn't know what to say, and I thought my role as the head of the classroom was to share what I knew, to speak and to be heard. It left me exhausted after each class. Like I'd run out of words.

My second year of teaching, I wanted to reorganize the flow of each class's rhythm. I thought back to my own college days, and a professor who would give us a free-write question to respond to. It was always a simple question, and she would give us two to five minutes to write a response. Sometimes we shared, other times we didn't.

I thought I'd bring that to my classroom, so the first day of my second year of teaching, we started with free-writes—one question each day, and they had two minutes to respond.

As you can imagine, the first couple of days, I got eyerolls and laughs. I'm sure they thought writing about themselves was a waste of time. But what we'd do afterward was share—anyone who wanted to share what they wrote could, if they wanted. There was never any pressure to do so, but the more we got into the school year, the longer the free-write and response sessions went. It was time to write and reflect, or write and listen, every single day. It really was a daily opportunity to train them to stop, pay attention, and listen.

When you set aside time daily to listen, you rewire your brain to turn off and just listen.

After teaching, I worked with a boss who had no ability to listen. She was a fast talker and a fast mover—constantly moving both physically and emotionally. She would often talk over you, or cut you off if you didn't talk fast enough. When she did stop to listen, it was maybe for a second, yet, you were never really sure if she was paying attention or seeking to understand what anyone was saying to her. Becoming a part of that environment was difficult because I never felt heard, but in an entirely different way than I was seeking from teaching. Because I knew the feeling of not being heard, I vowed that I would never make someone else feel like they weren't heard—in work or in life.

I started to pay attention to people whom I felt were just not good listeners—and considering why. I was home in Pittsburgh one day, and I went on a date with a guy I knew from high school. We were driving to dinner, when he asked me where I wanted to go. I named the exact location.

"I don't really like that place, I think we should go here," he recommended.

So, we went where he wanted to go. I would never tolerate that now, but at the time, I did. I remember thinking, *Was I not clear?* But I knew in my gut that I was. He just didn't want to listen. Needless to say, that relationship didn't last long for the same reason that was evident that first date.

There are several levels of listening. First, there's listening for information. This is the world's most basic level of listening, so much so that it might be confused with hearing. We listen to understand or know the basics—whether they're facts or figures, dates or times. Then, there's listening to understand. This is the level where listening is a relationship with insight we need to respond to, to engage with, to support someone else. Then, there's listening between the lines—listening to what's said and what's unsaid.

I was working with a client recently, and we were hammering out facts and figures when I started to feel a shift in her body and her approach. Something felt off, like we were getting into uncomfortable territory. There was something happening in between the lines. Instead of plowing through, I stopped the conversation.

"I just want to do a temperature check," I said. "How are you feeling about this?"

After a pause, she looked at me and said, "I'm just not sure I'm ready for this stage."

It led to an entirely different conversation.

In the business world, we talk a lot about ecosystems.

An ecosystem in business is a network of organizations that are involved in the delivery of a service or product. This network can include suppliers or distributors, customers or competitors. The idea is that each entity in the ecosystem affects and is affected by the others in a way in which they're constantly evolving around and for each other.

As you can imagine, it's a throwback to the idea of the biological ecosystem—or a community or geographic area where plants, animals, and other organisms live and work together, in a sort of bubble. In the early twentieth century, we also started to use the word "ecosystem" to describe how nature cycles and flows. Really, how nature listens to and for itself.

As excited as we are today about ecosystems, we've always been thrilled by what they make possible. Our primal fascination with the most breathtakingly fresh meadow or awe-inspiring coral reef proves that.

The thing is, in both business and the environment, ecosystems only work to their fullest potential and expression when we let each player be exactly who they are, and we both pay attention and listen to them.

The classroom only works if everyone pays attention and listens.

The boardroom only works if everyone pays attention and listens.

The team only works if everyone pays attention and listens.

This is where and why listening becomes a three-dimensional experience. It only works if you show up ready to pay attention, seek to understand, and try to listen between the lines.

The three optimize and support together. But each time, it's listening that opens the door to the other two—and all that's possible.

When we listen together, we better understand who is at the table and the value and perspective they each bring. Ecosystems thrive when each contributor is heard and respected.

Even more so when they're given the space to flourish wildly for who they are.

We only get there by listening.

prompts for radical change

In case you missed it, this is about tuning in to how you listen and how you understand and live the levels of listening.

- When was the last time you really, truly listened?
- When have you listened between the lines?
- When are you not listening at all?
- How can listening more deeply help you personally or professionally?
- Who's a go-to listener in your life—and what makes them a good listener?

CHAPTER TEN:
show me the way

Right out of college, I started doing yoga. My high school French teacher was a part-time yoga instructor, so after graduating from college and moving home, I asked her how and where to go if I wanted to try it. I started slow, literally. With some slower flow, gentle yoga classes at a local Himalayan institute. When I moved from Pittsburgh to Charlotte in 2007, I found another class—a Monday evening class taught in an apartment complex's community room. I got hooked on the post-yoga feeling—this feeling I'd never had before—an epic combination of a sweaty workout with a meditative quality. I could easily just pass out into sleep after each workout. It was a juxtaposition that I needed at that point in my life.

I would eventually build up to hot yoga several times a week, before then working for **lululemon**, the international juggernaut in athletic apparel that started with yoga apparel in the early 2000s. I joined **lululemon** in Charlotte at a time when no one on the East Coast—outside of New York City—knew what **lululemon** was. All my friends and family knew was that I had left a relatively stable job teaching high school English at the tale-end of the 2009 recession to work for a yoga apparel company no one had ever heard of.

The role was a perfect combination of the support of a corporate retailer with a need for local, entrepreneurial spirit, which was something I knew I had in me but didn't quite understand how to channel. On a weekly basis, our small and mighty team of three exhausted ourselves at dozens of workout classes a week—from yoga to athletic conditioning—to peddle apparel to the Charlotte market before it was trendy. There were times we attended multiple yoga classes a day as part of a grassroots, hyper-local marketing strategy to spread the word about yoga, but really—athletic apparel.

I stopped doing yoga shortly after leaving **lululemon**—mainly because my love of the once peaceful practice was now commercialized for me. Really, what had changed was the intention. Yoga wasn't about yoga anymore. It was, in my mind and in my experience, a marketing tool.

Regardless of where I took yoga, whether it was gentle or hot, whoever the instructor was, there was something really grounding for me. It was the practice, no doubt, but it was more so the idea that every location, every teacher started classes with the idea of intention.

When I started yoga, I needed intention. I had graduated from college with no real plan—a lot of ideas and *what ifs*—but no solid plan, no exact direction or intention. I didn't realize that the concept of intention or setting an intention was part of the yoga practice. So, when I started simple, one-hour yoga practices, I found myself subconsciously exploring the idea of intention. Going to a yoga class where an instructor laid out an intention for the class was exactly what I needed at that time in my life. Whether it was a word, a quote, or the flow to come, the idea of intention made sense to me. In this sense, intention is the gentlest form of strategy you'll ever learn—there's a plan of action guiding the movement to come.

As I started my career, I began to confuse the idea of intention with the idea of expectation—or an attachment to an outcome. They're two very different concepts that can get easily confused for the other when we're in stressful situations. Suddenly, the idea of intention—something done on purpose, deliberately, but with some beautiful nuances and flow—wasn't enough. It had to be about *how* it's done, or the expectation.

Often, that confusion is activated when we're in situations where perfectionism takes over. Simple intentions get hijacked by the expectation of what you think it should be, and suddenly, the intention to get through a yoga class becomes more about how it's done, or even worse, how it's done as compared to someone else.

I remember vividly when I was teaching a yearbook class, and one of our student editors printed out several pages for me to review. What started as a simple intention—to review pages and provide edits to a teenage editor—became about me spotting errors everywhere. The intention had been hijacked by my expectation, but never communicated.

I remember saying out loud to a classroom of students, "This has to be perfect."

I stopped myself after I heard myself say it. The intention to teach had been hijacked by this expectation that no mistakes were allowed. I tried to never use the word "perfect" again when teaching. That's about as far from the intention as you can get.

This same feeling of intention versus expectation is activated a lot in business ownership.

Whether you're one year into a business, or ten years in, people will ask what your goal was when you started the business. In my understanding of this question as both the receiver of the question and an observer when others are asked, business owners oftentimes stumble through this question. This is because the intention changes—it morphs over time because you, the business owner, morph over time. The intention on day one is different than the intention today. And it should be.

toth shop is named for Erzsébet Toth who, at just 19, left her home in the village of Paczin, Hungary, to board a transatlantic ship in the Belgian port city of Antwerp on May 23, 1912.

She was escaping an arranged marriage, and what we think were perhaps the early and hushed rumblings of World War 1 in Eastern Europe.

She did it by herself, in the middle of the night. Her ship docked at Ellis Island in New York City on June 4, 1912. She spoke no English; she knew no one in America; she had very little money. That intention—to start a new life in a new country—was familiar to millions of people during that era of history.

Each time that intention was set, and that drastic move was made, it changed the course of history for a family, while reinventing stories and legacies forever.

In her case, she made her way from New York City to Pittsburgh, where there was a strong Hungarian population. She married Josef Doczy; she became a mother to two boys. Sometime during the 1920s, she went back to Hungary for a visit with her two sons. From what we can tell, her intention might have shifted. She might have been considering moving her family—and the money made in America—back to Hungary. The three traveled to Hungary by boat, again through Ellis Island—but they ended up returning to America.

And in 1957, Elizabeth Toth Doczy became a United States citizen.

That story means a lot to me because "Toth" is my middle name. I'm named for her, my maternal great-grandmother. From our family search, we think her original intention was to come to America, make enough money, to then go back. Many families who came through Ellis Island had that same thought. But sometimes, the intention changes with circumstance, experience, and flexibility.

Setting a goal with flexibility and without self-judgment is damn hard, if not impossible... or is it?

Ironically enough, one of the pieces of working for **lululemon**, meant we were asked to write goals—one-year, five-year, and ten-year goals. The one-year goals always felt easy and snackable; the five-year and ten-year goals always felt hard because a person doesn't necessarily have a clear idea who they'll be one year, two years, or five years from today.

What if I put these ten-year goals in a time capsule, open it a decade later, and feel disappointed?

I remember a customer coming into our **lululemon** store one time and reading the goals that were posted back by the fitting rooms. I was helping people swap clothes in and out, when he turned to me, and said: "What if your ten-year goal isn't to work for this company—do they not promote you?"

It was a fair question from an outsider's perspective.

How do you adjust your intentions and goals over time?

For me, what changed over time was the idea of who sets the intention, which I found to be one of the things I craved in business ownership. I felt like, over the course of my career, I moved from the intention being set for me, to me setting my own intention.

An entrepreneurial-minded person setting your own intention is both a blessing and a curse.

How'd that happen?

It comes with time and experience. It also comes when you work for or with enough people who don't have any intention. Through that contrast, you might start to see and feel that you do have more intention than you realized.

Setting intentions is hard work. You're calling yourself and others to clear the clutter, to focus, to come up with what you think is a gentle strategy but is really a drive to move forward through a practice, a day, a business.

When I choose to be intentional, it never goes wrong. Even if it's not exactly as I envisioned, there are always more positives than negatives. Because I'm putting blinders on my brain. I'm training myself how to move through *something, anything.*

If I can compare it to anything, it's bowling with guardrails up. When you set an intention, there's a path, with lots of space, a clear destination, and some way to avoid sliding into the gutters.

In early 2023, I had lunch with a dear minister friend. As we sat and ate and talked about life, I started to ask him God and faith questions. As I floated around the idea of my upcoming fortieth birthday, I asked him how you know you're living into your purpose, i.e., the purpose, or intention God has for your life.

How do you know you're doing what God wants you to do?

"Ask Him to show you the way," he said.

Then he turned to the window we were sitting beside, and said, "God, show her the way," before returning his attention to our soups and salads.

Since that day, the idea of intention has been clear, really simple—it's both an ask of a higher power and the idea that I show up to do the work.

prompts for radical change

In case you missed it, this is a conversation about how you set intentions. There's a textbook definition for the word "intention" ("a thing intended; an aim or plan") and then there's your own definition of intention. (Yes, Virginia, you do get to define your own intention.)

- How do you define intention?
- What has informed or shaped that definition of intention?
- What's your relationship with intention?
- What's intention versus expectation like in your life?
- What's your intention today?

EASY NEXT STEPS

get your prompts for radical change answers moving

The cover of this book is a good example of how much spaces change over time with water and light—or, as I like to think of it, *movement and insight.* People are the same way—we change with *movement and insight* all the time.

Be open to revisiting and reading your responses to your prompts every couple of months—or maybe every year—to see how you have shifted or changed.

Bonus points: Your responses to these prompts might also make for great blog posts or social media posts; OR, if anything, they might be your messy first draft to great content to come.

Your responses to these prompts can be private or can be transformed into more consumable content, if you so choose.

start a note in your phone to capture insights

We sometimes think aha! moments come in big moments—graduations, birthdays, work milestones. And they absolutely do. *You Are Something New* moments also come in the everyday moments—traffic, emails, quick trips, good moments, or challenging conversations.

Start a note in your phone to capture moments or experiences and maybe one aha! moment or lesson you learned from it. It doesn't have to be a big lesson - micro lessons can also have a big impact as they can shift how you show up for the world.

keep learning

Pop over to megseitz.com for more quick tips to support your reading of *You Are Something New* and your journey, or read my blog "pep talks" for a quick dose of *something new* from me.

ABOUT THE AUTHOR

Meg Seitz is the founder and CEO of **toth shop**, a communications agency that focuses on a human, holistic approach to branding, marketing, and communications. Since 2014, the **toth shop** team has helped companies, c-suite leaders, and emerging brands articulate their expertise, talent, and value to the world by identifying storytelling gold nuggets that resonate with humans, as well as helping create compelling content and brand-building assets.

Over the last several years, Meg Seitz has taken in life lessons crossing the Carrick-a-Rede rope bridge in Northern Ireland, exploring the crystal caverns of Bermuda, seeing Vienna from the top of St. Stephen's Cathedral, and in places ranging from Jackson Hole to Sedona and Kennebunkport to Las Vegas.

Meg Seitz holds a bachelor of arts in English from Kenyon College and an MBA from Wake Forest University School of Business. She is a proud Double Drucker, meaning she placed twice in the top 10 (once in third place) for the international writing competition, the Peter Drucker Challenge. She is also proud to have been present in the audience to hear David Foster Wallace's "This is Water" commencement address live.

She lives in Charlotte, NC, with her fluffy corgi, Winnie, who recently passed therapy dog certification.

Connect with Meg at tothshop.com.

IG: @meg_seitz

LinkedIn: https://www.linkedin.com/in/megseitz/